BUILT FOR SUCCESS

THE STORY OF

# The NFL

Published by Creative Paperbacks
P.O. Box 227, Mankato, Minnesota 56002
Creative Paperbacks is an imprint of The Creative Company
www.thecreativecompany.us

DESIGN BY **ZENO DESIGN**
PRODUCTION BY **CHRISTINE VANDERBEEK**
ART DIRECTION BY **RITA MARSHALL**

Printed by Corporate Graphics in the United States of America

PHOTOGRAPHS BY Alamy (INTERFOTO), Corbis (Bettmann), Getty Images (ABC Photo Archives/ABC, Scott Boehm, Tom Dahlin, Hulton Archive, Kidwiler Collection/Diamond Images, Lambert, Kirby Lee, Al Messerschmidt, New York Times Co., NY Daily News Archive, Tony Triolo/Sports Illustrated, Jeff Zelevansky), Shutterstock (Mark Cinotti)



**THE LIBRARY OF CONGRESS HAS CATALOGED THE HARDCOVER EDITION AS FOLLOWS:**

Gilbert, Sara.
The story of the NFL / by Sara Gilbert.
p. cm. — (Built for success)
Includes bibliographical references and index.
Summary: A look at the origins, leaders, growth, and management of the NFL, the professional football league that was formed in 1920 and today governs 32 teams throughout the United States.
ISBN 978-1-60818-063-9 (hardcover)
ISBN 978-0-89812-661-7 (pbk)
1. National Football League—History—Juvenile literature.
2. Football—United States—History—Juvenile literature.
I. Title.

GV955.5.N35G55 2011
796.332'64—dc22 2010031224

CPSIA: 110310 P01382

First edition

9 8 7 6 5 4 3 2 1

BUILT FOR SUCCESS

THE STORY OF

# The NFL

SARA GILBERT

27
GU
63
27

Players for the Green Bay Packers and the Kansas City Chiefs were nervous on January 15, 1967. Vince Lombardi, the Packers' coach, trembled during a pregame television interview, and some Chiefs players were throwing up as they waited to run onto the field of the Los Angeles Memorial Coliseum. The two teams were playing in the first-ever Super Bowl (then known as the World Championship Game), a showdown between the best teams in the National Football League (NFL) and the rival American Football League (AFL). The NFL's Packers won 35–10, a triumph that earned each Green Bay player a $15,000 check; even the defeated Chiefs players of the AFL each took home $7,500. But the NFL received the best payoff: The annual Super Bowl soon became the most anticipated sporting event in the United States.

# CHAPTER ONE

# Only a Game

Professional football began in the U.S. in 1892, when the Allegheny Athletic Association in Allegheny, Pennsylvania, paid one of the players on its regional football club for a game. After that, amateur teams in towns on the East Coast and across the Midwest also began to pay their players.




Because there was no governing body to set and enforce rules for professional football, players jumped from team to team in search of the best salary. College players even joined such teams while they were still in school.

The lack of rules created not only confusion but also unfair advantages for wealthier team owners. So in the summer of 1920, representatives from four teams convened in the showroom of a car dealership in Canton, Ohio. Jim Thorpe, a former Olympic gold medalist in track and field who had gone on to star with professional baseball and football teams and was now a member of the Canton Bulldogs, wanted to discuss the formation of a league to govern the far-flung teams.

By mid-September, 14 teams from 4 states—including the Bulldogs, the Rochester (New York) Jeffersons, the Racine (Chicago, Illinois) Cardinals, and the Muncie (Indiana) Flyers—had agreed to participate in the new league, which would be called the American Professional Football Association (APFA). None of the charter

A renowned American Indian athlete, Jim Thorpe played for the Canton Bulldogs for six seasons

members actually paid the $100 fee that all had agreed would lend **credibility** to the APFA, though. Nevertheless, the teams were allowed to schedule their own games (including many against non-APFA teams), while the league established the rules that would govern games, teams, and their players.

By 1921, APFA membership stood at 22 teams, including the recently admitted Green Bay Packers. That year, the league named mechanic and Columbus Panhandles owner Joseph Carr as president. He soon moved the league's headquarters from Canton to Columbus, Ohio. Then he drafted a constitution to define territorial rights, set rules about when and why players could change teams, and establish league standings so that a clear champion from among the league's growing number of teams could be named at the end of each season. A year later, on June 24, 1922, the APFA changed its name to the National Football League, with Carr remaining as its president.

But the league was far from nationally recognized. Meager crowds attended most games, often leaving the teams—which were each responsible for their own expenses—struggling to break even. Then, in 1925, the Chicago Bears brought in college star Harold "Red" Grange, who had gained national recognition as a halfback at the University of Illinois. The **contract** he signed with the Bears brought recognition to the NFL, too. On Thanksgiving, he helped draw a record 36,600 fans to a scoreless game between the Bears and their crosstown rivals, the Chicago (formerly Racine) Cardinals. Grange drew fans everywhere the Bears played, including in New York, where Giants owner Wellington Mara was greatly relieved when 73,000 fans bought tickets to a Giants–Bears game, padding his team's bank account enough to keep it afloat.

That infusion of funds came just in time for the Giants. In 1927, Carr announced that the NFL would eliminate the 10 least financially stable **franchises**. A year later, two more teams disbanded. In 1933, the number of teams in the league stood at 10: the Bears (originally the Decatur Staleys), Cardinals, Giants, and Packers, along with the Boston Redskins (who would move to Washington

"The Galloping Ghost," Red Grange, drew attention to the young NFL with his spectacular running

in 1937), the Philadelphia Eagles, the Pittsburgh Pirates (who would become the Steelers in 1940), the Cincinnati Reds, the Brooklyn Dodgers, and the Portsmouth Spartans. Although the Reds, Dodgers, and Spartans would later disband, this group formed the nucleus of what would become the NFL of the future.

In 1933, the NFL divided its teams into two five-team divisions, with an annual championship game slated to be played between the top two teams from each division. Two years later, the league adopted the college draft, which Eagles owner Bert Bell promoted as the fairest way to disperse the pool of college players. Because Philadelphia had finished in last place the year before, the Eagles were given the first choice in the first draft, which was held in 1936. They chose Jay Berwanger, a University of Chicago halfback who had won the Heisman Trophy as college football's best player. Berwanger decided not to play in the NFL, however, making quarterback Riley Smith of the University of Alabama, who had been chosen by Boston with the number-two pick, the first player to actually sign and play. But like many other players of the era, Smith did not get rich off his contract with the Redskins. Most players earned less than $100 per game, and many worked regular jobs during the season as well.

The team owners themselves were losing more money in player salaries than they could bring in. "No owner has made money from pro football," Carr once said, "but a lot have gone broke thinking they could." There was no shortage of new owners willing to try. When the rival American Football League folded after just two seasons, at least three of the league's eight owners asked if they could join the NFL. In 1937, the NFL accepted the Cleveland Rams to replace the now-defunct Portsmouth Spartans. That was the last team that Carr welcomed into the NFL. On May 20, 1939, he suffered a heart attack and died.

> *"On any given Sunday, any team in our league can beat any other team.... You knock my brains out this Sunday, and I knock your brains out the next time we meet."*
>
> NFL COMMISSIONER BERT BELL

Football was a rough undertaking in the 1930s, as players (such as these Giants) wore little padding

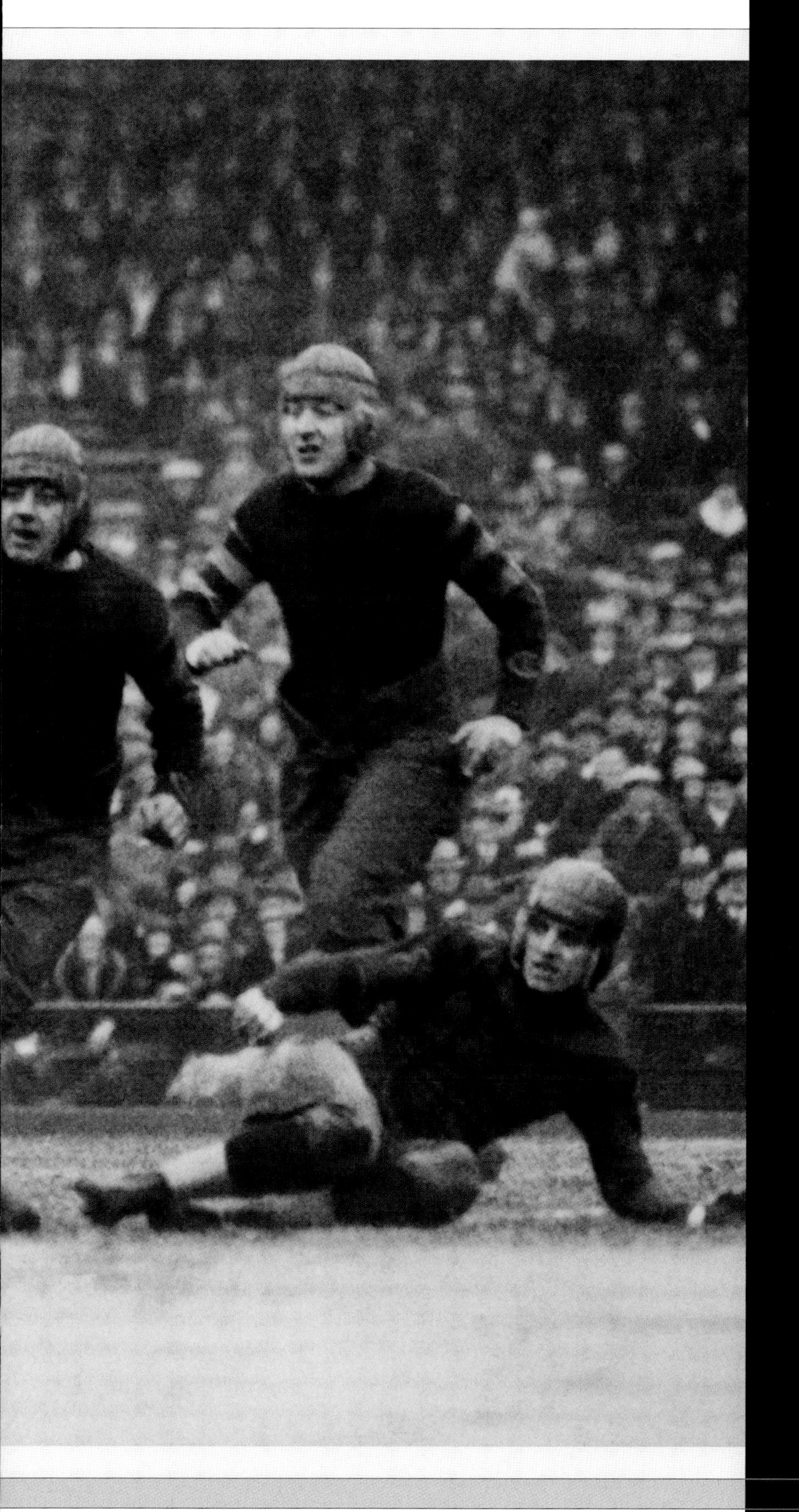

A 1925 Chicago Cardinals game

## CARDINAL CONTROVERSY

Early in NFL history, the team with the most wins during the season was awarded the title of league champion. In 1925, that team was the Chicago Cardinals. But the Pottsville (Pennsylvania) Maroons thought it should have been them. They had a 10–2 record, better than the Cardinals' 9–2–1 mark, and celebrated their championship with an exhibition game against a team of college All-Stars. League rules prohibited college players from competing in the NFL, however, and NFL president Joseph Carr suspended the Maroons for playing the unauthorized game. Carr then recognized two pickup games the Cardinals had played to push their record to 11–2–1. Pottsville fans protested the decision for decades, even after the team disbanded. In 2003, the NFL voted against reversing its decision. "[Pottsville] was a championship-caliber team that ran into an unfortunate conflict with the league's rules," NFL commissioner Paul Tagliabue said. "At this late date, it was impossible to overturn."

# CHAPTER TWO

# Saved by the Bell

The first person to replace Carr as president was NFL cofounder Carl Storck, a large man who presided over meetings while nibbling on boxes of chocolates. The team owners weren't impressed and tried to entice others—including J. Edgar Hoover, who at the time was director of the FBI—to take the position.



Storck resigned the position in 1941 and was replaced by Elmer Layden, a former star fullback and coach for the University of Notre Dame.

Most of Layden's decisions, including a new rule that game officials wear brightly colored uniforms to indicate their role on the field, were overshadowed by the country's entry into World War II just as he became the NFL's first **commissioner** and moved the league's headquarters to Chicago. By May 1942, 112 of 346 total players had been **drafted** into the military. So few players were available that, in 1943, the Pittsburgh Steelers and Philadelphia Eagles joined forces and temporarily became known as the "Steagles." Other teams found their own ways to field complete rosters. "We held tryouts at Cubs Park," Bears owner George Halas said, "and signed up anybody who could run around the field twice." By the time the war ended in 1945, 638 NFL players had fought overseas, and 21 had died in action.

George Halas, who served in both World Wars I and II, owned the Chicago Bears for 63 years

After the war, a new battle began at home, this one between the NFL and the eight-team All-America Football **Conference** (AAFC), which was founded in 1946 by a group of wealthy investors upset over the NFL's refusal to expand to the West Coast. (The NFL was unwilling to burden its teams with the expense of traveling so far.)

Many team owners were disappointed with the way Layden had handled the emergence of the AAFC. They voted to fire him and to hire Eagles co-owner and coach Bert Bell as the next NFL commissioner. At Bell's first official meeting in his new role, the owners of the Cleveland Rams lobbied to move their team to Los Angeles—both to avoid competition with the AAFC's powerful Cleveland Browns and to stake a claim in California, where the AAFC had established two teams.

When NFL owners voted against the move, Rams owner Dan Reeves vowed to leave the NFL if the decision stood. Eventually, Bell brokered a deal that worked for everyone: The Rams could move if Reeves paid each visiting team $5,000 to help cover travel costs, in addition to the $10,000 home teams were already required to pay visiting teams. Reeves agreed.

With that fight settled, Bell moved league headquarters to Philadelphia, where he quietly addressed the AAFC issue. His official strategy was to not discuss the rival league. But even if he ignored it, the rest of the nation did not. The AAFC and its perennial champion, the Browns, stole most of the football headlines in 1946 and 1947.

Ironically, the Browns' dominance soon did the AAFC in. When the Browns won all 14 of their games in 1948, fans were so bored that attendance plummeted around the league. The competition in the NFL, meanwhile, was heating up, and fans were coming out in greater numbers than ever. So in December 1949, the two leagues announced a **merger**: three AAFC teams—the Browns, San Francisco 49ers, and Baltimore Colts—would join the NFL in 1950, while the other four would be dissolved.

*"I believe in the star system. It's the only thing that sells tickets. It's what you put on the stage or playing field that draws people."*

SONNY WERBLIN, FORMER MANAGING PARTNER OF THE NEW YORK JETS

As leader of the dominant Browns, Cleveland quarterback Otto Graham was a 1940s football icon

Bell considered the merger a personal triumph. But he still had to find a way for the NFL to start making money, since teams continued to spend more than they could make in ticket sales. Although the first televised football game had been aired in 1939, Bell didn't believe that a new medium was the answer. Broadcasting games, he reasoned, would take fans out of the stands. In 1950, when the Los Angeles Rams accepted a $75,000 fee from the Admiral Television Company to broadcast all of its games locally, his theory was proven correct. Attendance in Los Angeles dropped by almost 50 percent that year; Admiral, which had agreed to make up for any lost ticket sales, was forced to pay the Rams $307,000.

By 1951, however, national broadcasts were possible, and the NFL Championship Game between the Rams and Browns was aired from coast to coast. In 1956, Bell reluctantly acknowledged that television could be good for the league and allowed the Columbia Broadcasting System (CBS) to broadcast select regular-season games—but banned broadcasting home games within the home team's **market**. "I don't believe there is any honesty in selling a person a ticket and then, after you've taken his dollar, deciding to put the game on television," Bell said in 1957. "As long as I have anything to do with this league, home games won't be televised, period."

Just a year later, however, he allowed the NFL Championship Game between the Giants and Colts to be broadcast nationally, including in New York City, where the game was played. More than 64,000 fans filled the stadium to capacity, and another 45 million watched the dramatic finale of the game on television. Bell was amazed—and enlightened. But he wouldn't live to see television's total impact on the game; on October 11, 1959, Bell died of a heart attack while sitting in the stands of an Eagles-Steelers contest.

The 1958 NFL Championship Game (won by the Colts, 23–17) has been called "The Greatest Game Ever Played"

REMINGTON RAND
REMINGTON

Bert Bell announcing suspensions in 1947

## GAMBLING ON GAMES

NFL commissioner Bert Bell wasn't pleased when he got a call from the mayor of New York City the night before the 1946 championship game. Two New York Giants players were being questioned for attempting to influence the outcome of the game via dishonest play. Bell suspended both players, who admitted to the fix, then tried to make sure it would never happen again. He hired retired police officers to keep an eye on the players and instituted new rules, including injury reports detailing who likely would and wouldn't be playing each week, to prevent players from taking themselves out of the lineup at the last minute. "Professional football cannot continue to exist unless it is based on absolute honesty," Bell said. But almost 20 years later, new commissioner Pete Rozelle also had to deal with gambling when Green Bay's Paul Hornung and Detroit's Alex Karras were caught betting on games. Both were suspended indefinitely but later allowed back in the league.

# CHAPTER THREE

# Rozelle's Reign

Alvin Ray "Pete" Rozelle was only 33 years old when he replaced Bell as NFL commissioner in January 1960 and moved the league's headquarters to New York. Rozelle had started working for the Rams as an assistant to the **public relations** manager and advanced to become general manager of the team by 1957. He had helped turn that club into a financial success, and he hoped to have the same impact on the league.

Rozelle recognized that selling television rights could be the key to making money in the NFL. But first, he had to clean up the cluttered television contracts that teams had independently negotiated with different networks. He also had to convince the owners to share the income that would stem from having a joint television contract—not an easy sell among teams in cities with a larger audience, such as the Giants, who were already making almost 10 times more from television contracts than teams in smaller towns such as Green Bay, Wisconsin. Distributing the **profits** would guarantee steady income for each team, no matter how well it played, Rozelle contended, and such a policy would also build

Thanks largely to television, the NFL saw its audience grow dramatically in the early 1960s

better competition by helping more teams afford talented players.

The next obstacle was negotiating a contract that didn't violate antitrust laws, which help ensure fair competition within industries. Rozelle went to Washington, D.C., for assistance with that part. On September 30, 1961, president John F. Kennedy signed the Sports Broadcasting Act into law, exempting professional sports leagues from laws that prohibited them from doing business with just one network. Three months later, the NFL inked its first national contract with CBS, which agreed to pay $4.65 million annually for two years to broadcast regular-season games; the National Broadcasting Company (NBC), meanwhile, maintained the rights to air the championship game.

Every two years, when the contract with CBS was up for renewal, Rozelle managed to increase the fee. In 1964, CBS paid the NFL $28.2 million for 2 years; in 1966, the rate was hiked 25 percent to $37.6 million. As the networks began competing for the rights, it became easier to increase the rates—and to broadcast more games. The advent of Monday Night Football on the American Broadcasting Company (ABC) network in 1970 brought in extra revenue as well. By 1974, the NFL was earning $63 million a year for national broadcast rights—and more than half of that was distributed to the teams.

But Rozelle had more to deal with than just network negotiations. There was also the matter of the new American Football League (AFL), which had been founded in 1959 after the NFL rejected the Chicago Cardinals' bid to relocate to Dallas and expand the league. The AFL fielded eight teams, including some in cities located near NFL teams, creating direct competition for fans in those areas. And because the AFL had negotiated a shared television contract before the NFL, it had the financial stability to survive where earlier rival leagues had not.

The war between the NFL and AFL reached a climax in 1966. Although the supply of players was growing as college football became more popular, there was still fierce competition for the top talents. In 1966, NFL and AFL teams

Don Meredith (left) and Howard Cosell (right) were part of the original Monday Night Football broadcasting team

spent a combined $7 million signing players. That spike in salaries pushed some teams to the brink financially and helped propel a series of secret meetings to discuss joining forces. On June 8, 1966, Rozelle announced a merger between the NFL and AFL that would integrate all 24 existing franchises into 1 league—the NFL—with 2 conferences: the American Football Conference (AFC) and the National Football Conference (NFC). Teams from the NFL and AFL would begin playing against each other during the 1970 season, but the top teams from each league would meet for a World Championship Game—later known as the Super Bowl—beginning in 1967.

The united league flourished. Surveys in the 1970s showed that more Americans enjoyed professional football than professional baseball, and the annual Super Bowl had become the most popular sporting event in the U.S., setting new records for viewership almost every year. The sport's increasing popularity also enabled the NFL to branch out, **licensing** clothing and other team-related merchandise through NFL Properties beginning in 1963 and creating documentary programs about the different teams and their games through NFL Films beginning in 1964.

But all was not rosy for Rozelle. On July 1, 1974, the NFL Players Association (NFLPA), the **union** representing NFL players, went on **strike**, and players began **picketing** training camps. The owners had become rich from television revenues and ticket sales, but the players felt that they weren't receiving a fair share of the wealth, since the average player's salary had not topped $30,000.

The NFLPA presented the owners with a list of 93 demands, including a request for free agency, which would allow players to negotiate with other teams when their contracts with their current team ended. They also sought guaranteed salaries, which would be paid even if players were hurt and couldn't play. The strike lasted until August 29, when the players finally gave up and reported to training camp. They were getting paid to play football, but they had made little headway on their long list of demands.

*"There are more women becoming avid fans of the NFL than any other sport. What they love is that it's the one time of the week that the family all gets together."*

SUSAN ROTHMAN, VICE PRESIDENT OF CONSUMER PRODUCTS FOR THE NFL

Sales of merchandise, including replica jerseys, has long been a big moneymaker for NFL franchises

SUPER BOWL XLIV
SONY
COLTS

FOOTBALL ON FILM

For years, Ed Sabol had used the 16-millimeter camera he got as a wedding gift to film everything he could, including his son's football games. But in 1961, as he watched footage from the NFL Championship Game, Sabol thought he could make a better film. In 1962 he convinced commissioner Pete Rozelle to pay him $3,000 to shoot the championship game between the Green Bay Packers and New York Giants. Although his fingers were frozen by the end of the December contest, Sabol produced a 28-minute film compiled from shots taken at such creative angles (cameramen lay on the ground and even climbed into the rafters of the stadium) that Rozelle hired him to do it again. In 1964, Rozelle brought Sabol's company, Blair Motion Pictures, in-house to help promote the league, renaming it NFL Films. Sabol and his son Steve, who wrote the scripts for the films, were part of the package. One *New York Times* writer called Sabol "the most underrated filmmaker working today."

# CHAPTER FOUR

# Strike Two, Strike Three

The players returned to the field in 1974 without a new contract from the league—one was not signed until 1977, in fact, after the NFLPA filed a lawsuit against the owners, forcing them to meet a few of the players' demands. The agreement made in 1977 included an increase in the minimum salary, along with improved health benefits, and gave players more freedom to sign with other teams when their contracts ended.

When the 1977 contract expired in 1982, the average annual salary for an NFL player was $90,000. Although star players were receiving much more, many others were receiving much less. Quarterbacks could earn up to $160,000, while kickers averaged $65,000. But the owners were making millions. Attendance at NFL games had topped 13.6 million in 1981, an average of more than 560,000 fans throughout the league per week, and the television networks were enjoying all-time high ratings for their game broadcasts. In light of this, the NFLPA suggested that the players should receive a larger percentage of the league's **gross revenue** in their new contracts.

The NFLPA had learned that striking during training camp didn't put any pressure

With injury always a possibility in football, the NFLPA has fought for expanded health benefits

on the owners, who didn't lose money if their players didn't practice. But the owners would lose substantial revenue if games weren't played. In 1982, a strike was called at midnight on September 20, with the regular season already in progress. The strike lasted 57 days and cut the season short by 8 games (only 1 was made up). But in the end, it was again the NFLPA that gave in, accepting an offer that was less than the players had requested. The owners agreed to an escalating minimum wage scale that started at $30,000 for rookies and went up to $200,000 for 18-year veterans, but they did not set a specific percentage of the league's gross revenue aside for salaries.

The labor battle was just one issue that soured the mood of the usually amiable Rozelle in 1982. The year had also been marred by the revelation that several players had been using or selling drugs such as cocaine and marijuana. The *New York Daily News* published a five-part series about the drug problems in the NFL, alleging that 50 percent of the league's players had used cocaine at some point. Five players were **suspended** for drug-related charges in 1982, damaging not only their careers but also the reputation of the league as a whole. The *Daily News* reported that Rozelle was "highly concerned with [the NFL's] image."

In the midst of the drug disgrace, Al Davis, the owner of the Oakland Raiders, won a lawsuit against the NFL and earned the right to move his team to Los Angeles—a move that had previously required approval from the other owners in the league. Davis's victory not only set a precedent for teams hoping to relocate in the future but also opened the door for players to move from team to team more freely. The year had been so frustrating for Rozelle that during his annual press conference prior to the Super Bowl in January 1983, he told the media that 1982 had been a "very distasteful year for players, coaches, and owners of the National Football League."

The good news was that it had not affected the league's legions of fans. Super Bowl XVII, held on January 30, 1983, was the second-highest-rated live television program up to that time, with more than 40 million homes watching the

Redskins running back John Riggins was the star of Super Bowl XVII, rushing for a Super Bowl-record 166 yards

game. Two years later, the 1985 Chicago Bears recorded a video of the team's players singing and dancing to their rap song, "The Super Bowl Shuffle." More than 115 million people watched former Super Bowl standout Bart Starr (a Packers quarterback in the 1960s) perform the coin toss before Super Bowl XX, which the Bears won. As the number of viewers continued to increase, the Super Bowl became the biggest television event, live or recorded, of the year.

In 1987, the NFLPA came back to the owners to renegotiate player contracts—and again, disagreements over free agency led to a players' strike. But this time, the owners were the ones who had learned from what happened in 1982. When the strike was called on September 22, the league cancelled only the games scheduled for the following weekend. The next week, they brought in replacement players and paid them each the league-minimum of $3,125 a week. Although fewer fans watched the replacement games—either in person or on TV—the replacement players gave the owners the upper hand. Just 24 days into the strike, the players voted to return to their teams, with no settlement and no free agency.

Rozelle was disappointed with the whole process. He thought that bringing in replacement players diminished the credibility of the league, and he was tired of watching the same battle unfold like clockwork every five years. In the spring of 1989, he tearfully told the owners that he was retiring. The announcement was met with stunned silence, followed by a long, loud standing ovation. Only later, when the owners started talking about how to find a new commissioner, did the gravity of his retirement sink in. "We are searching for the replacement to an irreplaceable man," longtime Giants owner Wellington Mara said.

*"This league was based on people being partners and being together and helping out. It's one of the strong points of our league."*

DAN ROONEY,
OWNER OF THE PITTSBURGH STEELERS

NFL players on strike in 1987 resented replacement players, whom they derisively called "scabs"

## THE *HEIDI* HUBBUB

At 7:00 P.M. on November 17, 1968, with just 65 seconds left to play in a close game between the New York Jets and Oakland Raiders, NBC abruptly cut away from the game to start airing the movie *Heidi* instead. When the change happened, the Jets held a 3-point lead, 32–29. But fans who were forced to switch to watching the previously scheduled program missed the Raiders' improbable comeback, in which they scored two touchdowns on three plays and won 43–32. So many angry fans called NBC that the network's switchboards stopped working and circuits blew. At 8:40 P.M., those who were still watching *Heidi* saw news of the Raiders' win crawl across the bottom of the screen—which in turn interrupted one of the most dramatic moments in the movie. Jets quarterback Joe Namath later jokingly gave the movie a positive review. "I didn't see it," he said, "but I heard it was great."

# CHAPTER FIVE

# America's Game

Paul Tagliabue was shaving one October morning in 1989 when Rozelle called to officially offer the position of NFL commissioner to him. Tagliabue and his wife flew to Cleveland, where the owners were meeting, to accept the position and meet the media.



They flew back to their Washington, D.C., home later that night, where their daughter had another phone message for them. "Here's a phone number," she said. "[Former] President Reagan's in Japan, and he wants you to call him."

Such was the stature of the NFL when Tagliabue, a lawyer who had represented the NFL more than 50 times in 20 years, became commissioner in 1989. Much of that was a credit to what Rozelle had accomplished during his tenure with the league, but Tagliabue quickly made it clear that he was going to be his own leader. He wasn't afraid to fine owners and coaches when they made questionable decisions—including docking Cincinnati Bengals coach Sam Wyche a week's pay for refusing to allow a female reporter into the locker room. And he was also willing to try his hand at solving the still unresolved labor issues—particularly the demand for free agency—before they cut another season short.

During Paul Tagliabue's 17-year run as commissioner, the NFL expanded from 28 teams to 32

As contract negotiations heated up in 1992, a judge called both Tagliabue and NFLPA leaders to discuss a lawsuit that had been brought against the NFL by All-Pro defensive end Reggie White and other players seeking unrestricted free agency. The judge showed them an envelope and told them that neither side would like the solution that was sealed inside of it. He urged them to work together on a compromise.

Within days, the players and owners managed to solve the problem that had been haunting them for decades. The foundation of the **collective bargaining agreement** they signed in 1993 was a salary cap that set a limit on how much each team could spend on player wages (around 60 percent of the league's gross revenue, or about $34.6 million per team at the time). The NFL also offered every player unrestricted free agency after four years in the league.

Although not everyone was thrilled with the new agreement—some of the highest-paid players worried that it would limit their ability to demand more money—it brokered a long-term peace between owners and players and was followed by a prolonged period of prosperity for the NFL. In 1995, total attendance for all games topped 19 million for the first time, and in 2002 it went over the 21 million mark. The league had expanded in 1991 to include what is now known as NFL Europe, which fielded 10 teams in countries such as Germany, Spain, and the Netherlands. It also supported the Arena Football League, which was played with slightly different rules on smaller fields.

Revenues were skyrocketing for teams—in 1995, the average revenue per club in the NFL was more than $50 million. Player salaries claimed a large chunk of that, but owners still saw substantial profits, thanks in part to the longstanding income-sharing plan that Rozelle had put in place more than 40 years earlier. But some teams were finding new sources of revenue that didn't have to be shared—stadium naming rights, for example, and local radio and television deals. Teams in smaller markets worried that they wouldn't be able

A crowd of 98,374 packed the Rose Bowl in Pasadena, California, for Super Bowl XXVII in January 1993

to generate those funds and argued that the wealthier owners had an unfair advantage. As the owners tried to negotiate a new contract with the NFLPA in 2006, those concerns threatened to end the league's 17 consecutive years without a players' strike.

After spending two days locked in the ballroom of a hotel in Dallas, the owners and NFLPA representatives reached a deal, extending the 1993 collective bargaining agreement until 2011, with increases in the salary cap each year. And the owners agreed to tweak their revenue-sharing formula to keep small- and large-market teams on even footing with each other financially. In addition to the standard shared revenues, the 15 highest-earning teams would create a fund that could be used by lower-revenue teams as needed.

Not long after that contract was signed, the 65-year-old Tagliabue announced that he would retire at the end of July 2006. In August, Roger Goodell, who had started in the NFL as an **intern** in 1982, was named commissioner. "Roger got his MBA [Master of Business Administration] from Pete Rozelle and Paul Tagliabue," said New England Patriots owner Robert Kraft. "That's not a bad education."

Goodell had plenty of opportunities to test his knowledge of the league. By the end of the 2009 season, he was already fielding questions about the possibility of there not being a salary cap in 2010 because the owners had decided that they wanted to renegotiate the collective bargaining agreement. Although negotiations were slow to start, Goodell expressed optimism in early 2011 that a new agreement would be reached and that play would continue uninterrupted through 2011 and beyond.

For almost a century, the NFL has soldiered through far worse obstacles than lengthy negotiations. It has survived several rival leagues, three players' strikes, and dozens of lawsuits. The NFL's future as America's favorite professional sport appears to be bright, thanks to the lessons that have been learned during its long and storied history.

> *"We [NFL teams] compete against each other for three hours a week. Otherwise, we have aligned interests."*
>
> ROBERT KRAFT, OWNER OF THE NEW ENGLAND PATRIOTS

As commissioner, Roger Goodell quickly earned a reputation as a no-nonsense disciplinarian

LOSING A LEADER

When 33-year-old Pete Rozelle accepted the position of NFL commissioner in 1960, he was told that he would grow into the job. And he did. He became known as one of the greatest leaders in all of professional sports. But the stress of the job took a toll on his health. By the 1980s, the rigors of the work—especially the ongoing labor disputes—led him to smoke three packs of cigarettes a day and kept him from sleeping. "I saw more frowns on Pete's face in the 1980s than I'd seen in all the years before that put together," said sportswriter and longtime friend Don Weiss. By 1987, the situation was so dire that Rozelle suffered a small stroke. He retired in 1989 and died on December 6, 1996, not long after being diagnosed with a brain tumor. A few weeks later, at Super Bowl XXXI, the players honored his memory by putting "Pete" stickers on their helmets.

# GLOSSARY



**collective bargaining agreement** a legally enforced contract between the management of an organization and its employees, which establishes the conditions of employment, including wages, working hours, and benefits

**commissioner** the head of a professional sports organization who is responsible for overseeing the operations of that organization

**conference** a group of teams within a sports league

**contract** a legally binding agreement between two people or two parties

**credibility** the ability to be believed and respected

**drafted** selected to join a team or organization, such as the military

**franchises** professional sports teams that are part of a larger league

**gross revenue** the total income earned by a company, without subtracting any expenses

**intern** an advanced student or graduate who works, with supervision, in a professional position to gain experience in a certain field

**licensing** granting permission for the use of trademarked, patented, or other individually owned products or services

**market** a region where the population can see or hear the same television or radio broadcasts of a certain team's games, or the area that encompasses what is considered to be the team's "home"

**merger** the combining of two or more entities into one through a purchase or a pooling of interests

**picketing** marching or standing in front of an office or other venue as an act of protest, often during a strike, or work stoppage

**profits** the amount of money that a business keeps after subtracting expenses from income

**public relations** the practice of establishing and maintaining a favorable connection between a company and the public

**strike** a work stoppage that takes place to protest an employer's policies or to support a specific bargaining position

**suspended** temporarily banned from a specific activity, privilege, or position, usually as a form of punishment

**union** an organization of workers who join together to protect their common interest and to improve the conditions of their employment, including wages and hours

# SELECTED BIBLIOGRAPHY

MacCambridge, Michael. *America's Game: The Epic Story of How Pro Football Captured a Nation.* New York: Random House, 2004.

Maule, Tex. *The Game: The Official Picture History of the NFL.* New York: Random House, 1964.

NFL Enterprises. "History of the NFL." National Football League. http://www.nfl.com/history.

Oates, Bob Jr., ed. *The First Fifty Years: A Celebration of the National Football League in Its Fiftieth Season.* New York: Simon and Schuster, 1969.

Oriard, Michael. *Brand NFL: Making and Selling America's Favorite Sport.* Chapel Hill: University of North Carolina Press, 2007.

Pro Football Hall of Fame. "History of Pro Football." Pro Football Hall of Fame. http://www.profootballhof.com/history.

Yost, Mark. *Tailgating, Sacks, and Salary Caps: How the NFL Became the Most Successful Sports League in History.* Chicago: Kaplan Publishing, 2006.

# INDEX